A Gift

To _____

_____

From _____

_____

_____

_____

_____

_____

Acknowledgements

I am grateful for the gifts of words and thoughts in this book from Sally Baker, Dan Barbiero, Jess Bossung, Mary Ellen Fahs, Johnnie Freeman, Phyllis Fritts, Kathy Genovese, Polly Greenberg, B Hanson, Sara Hall, Carlotta Hartmann, Mary Jo Hossfeld, Susan Lassen, Robin London, Joan Long, Kay Macy, Lucy Masterman, Joyce McGill, Amy Phillipps, Liz Powers, Samuel Powers, Stephen Price, Barbara Rogus, Priscilla Ruffin, Lee Rushmore, Rabbi Jeffrey K. and Nina Salkin, Judy Smith, Nancy Freeman Soward, Adm. James Stockdale, Carol Swiggett, Jeanie Tengelsen, Barbara Towers, Alison Tung, Bob, Jenifer, and Rob Walton, Carolyn Watson, Joan Wiles, and Owen Youngquist, and all who read the manuscript and said "Do the book!" For their good and generous skills in illustration and design, I particularly thank Byrdie Platt and Inger Gibb.

Pages vi, 60 From *For You Departed* by Alan Paton. Copyright © 1969 by Alan Paton. Used with permission of Scribner, a Division of Simon & Schuster, Inc. ▪ 9 "Wild Geese" from *Dream Work* © 1986 by Mary Oliver. Used by permission of the author and Grove/Atlantic, Inc. ▪ 20 From *Gates of Repentance, The New Union Prayerbook for Days of Awe,* used with permission from Central Conference of American Rabbis, New York, Revised 1996. ▪ 22 From *Snow Falling on Cedars* © 1995 by David Guterson. Used with permission from Harcourt, Inc. ▪ 38 From THE POETRY OF ROBERT FROST, edited by Edward Connery Lathem © 1942 by Robert Frost, 1969 by Henry Holt and Company, 1970 by Lesley Frost Ballantine. Reprinted by permission of Henry Holt and Company, LLC. ▪ 45 From "If It Be Thy Will," by Ben Ludlow, from music of St. John's Church, Cold Spring Harbor, New York. ▪ 47 From the LETTERS OF RAINER MARIA RILKE: 1892-1910 translated by Jane Bannard Greene and M. D. Herter Norton. Copyright 1945 by W. W. Norton & Company, Inc., renewed © 1972 by M. D. Herter Norton. Used by permission of W. W. Norton & Company, Inc.

Library of Congress Control Number 2001118805 ▪ ISBN 0-9711869-0-1

Kindnesses

A journey through the seasons of grief –
Poems, prayers, and joyous observations

By Terry Walton

Illustrations by Byrd Platt

Rosalie Ink Publications

Cold Spring Harbor, NY

"When words are wished for, silence hurts my heart."

– Rosalie Slack

"I pray that God will soften the hard edges of this for you -
with friends who love you and gentle things happening."

– From a friend

Dedication

To Seymour, Charles, Mariamne, Hal, and our families,
who lost Elizabeth too. To my dear and generous-hearted
friends. To Bon. And to all who loved Doug.

And, as this book goes to press,
to the September 11 families, friends, and rescuers.

"Death is nothing at all.
I have only slipped into the next room.
I am I and you are you.
Whatever we were to each other that we are still."

– Canon Henry Scott-Holland
1847-1913

"Something within me is waking from long sleep, and I want
to live and move again. Some zest is returning to me, some
immense gratefulness for those who love me, some strong
wish to love them also. I am full of thanks for life. I have not
told myself to be thankful, I just am so."

– Alan Paton

Contents

Introduction 3

Who Was It I Lost? 5

Fall 7

Your Place in the Family of Things ▪ The Windowsill of Heaven
Bird Mindfulness ▪ Indian Summer ▪ Night Wings ▪ Fox
Island Quality ▪ Ant

Winter 19

The Tree of Lights ▪ Whither From Here ▪ All Is Well ▪ Morning
Long Island December ▪ Crossing the Street ▪ Forsythia Is Fooled
Sun Up ▪ Snow in March

Spring 33

Skateboarding ▪ Easter Letter ▪ Samuel's Poem ▪ Where Is Your Garden,
Anyway? ▪ Silken Ties ▪ April ▪ Rushing By ▪ Blessings

Summer 43

God Keep You, Dearest ▪ Give Me Understanding ▪ Lord, Slow Me Down

The Pictures Within You ▪ The Rock Club ▪ Good Night's Sleep
"I will hold you in my thoughts"

Fall, & Full Circle 51

Two Journeys ▪ Brother and Sister ▪ The Time to Say Love
Those Who Have Finished Their Work in This Life ▪ A Birthday
October Sunday ▪ Puppies ▪ The Linen Closet ▪ Summer Church

Journey Through the Seasons of Grief 62

Kindnesses 64

Introduction

Mine was the dearest of sisters, our minds so close that we invariably said "I was just about to call you!" when one of us telephoned the other. Separately and together we reached a good mid-life time, Elizabeth and I, a time after children were grown and gone, a time sharing discovery and delight. ❦ At her death from cancer six years ago there were many kindnesses shown me – a flower on the doorstep, a poem or a prayer, or simply the dear gift of listening. At that time too I began to notice, as if with new eyes, the sweet details of my natural and neighborly surroundings. ❦ For that year and some time beyond, I kept a journal of my sister's progression through illness toward death. It was a journal of my own rage and tears intermixed, paradoxically and blessedly, with times of joy. It was a refuge from the intensities of unwanted and awful knowledge, as we moved through the unthinkable. It lent solace at any hour of dark or light. ❦ And now at last comes a glimmer of understanding. These kind acts, these inter-connections of reality and spirit, are mysterious and nourishing evidence that we are all part of a bigger picture than we know. *Kindnesses,* which comes from my journal, reflects two parts of a single journey: the gifts that I received in the seasons of sadness, and the grateful observations I made - illumined by the context of their time - of my ordinary, beautiful surroundings. TW

"I believe that friends are quiet angels
who lift us to our feet when our wings have
trouble remembering how to fly."

Anonymous

Who Was It I Lost?

Who was it I lost? A companion in childhood – who admired the sole-shaped Roman sandals I cut from shirt cardboards and colored yarns, criss-cross laced up to my little knees and worn with pride.

Who held flashlights angled under the broken plaster-lathed floorboards of our old house with me, down on hands and knees and face to the floor, seeking missing marbles or a prior generation's hidden treasures. Surely they must be there.

In whose room our brother and I made warm quilt-beds on the wooly old rug, listening to the Green Hornet and the Lone Ranger by radio at bedtime, thrilling to chases and feeling utterly content.

We were four years apart, my sister and I. We fought bickeringly with each other or our brother, depending on the occasion, played tag in the dark with neighborhood friends, later as teenagers shared a room yet led pretty separate lives. When she went away to Switzerland to study, I feeling bereft as an unnoticed younger sister, she made me a card of flowers pasted together from patterned cloths – tiny Swiss flowers white on blue, white on lime green. Somewhere I still have this beloved present.

Later but before our marriages, I would realize that of the two sisters, I had traveled the far easier path, the third child of three, the follower on a blazed trail. And I would realize that even with cheery-light voice she was by nature both responsible and vulnerable, and both extremely. She arranged each detail of my wedding because our mother had died, responded patiently to my new-wife and new-mother questions over the years, sent wonderful hand-me-downs for our children and equally wonderful advice. And in our middle lives, not too many years ago, at Stonehenge, the sky red-gold and the colossal stones in silhouette, she wondered with me at all that had gone before.

She loved clothes and silver things, my sister. She gave fanciful presents and was playful – sending mystery valentines to our children and her own, somehow postmarked in faraway cities. She was brown-haired and brown-eyed, slim-waisted and full-hipped, and meticulous in all her ways – sometimes overly so like me.

She listened compassionately, ranted appropriately when angry, treasured an artist's sculpted scene of Colorado's Mesa Verde cave dwellers that she found with her husband and kept in their front hall. Coming home from work each day she would oftentimes say, checking for the blinking green light of telephone messages, "Let's see if anybody loves us!" She bought a southwestern desert painting with a rainbow in it even after her sentence of death, or perhaps because of it.

My brother Hal,
my sister Elizabeth,
myself.

Fall

Your Place in the Family of Things

This poem came from a friend with whom I have shared great hilarity in good times, and each other's shoulders at other times. It was written by Mary Oliver and for me its last five lines, beginning "Whoever you are, no matter how lonely . . ." lifted the isolation that sadness brings.

Wild Geese

You do not have to be good.
You do not have to walk on your knees
for a hundred miles through the desert, repenting.
You only have to let the soft animal of your body
  love what it loves.
Tell me about despair, yours, and I will tell you mine.
Meanwhile the world goes on.
Meanwhile the sun and the clear pebbles of the rain
are moving across the landscapes,
over the prairies and the deep trees,
the mountains and the rivers.
Meanwhile the wild geese, high in the clean blue air,
are heading home again.
Whoever you are, no matter how lonely,
the world offers itself to your imagination,
calls to you like the wild geese, harsh and exciting —
over and over announcing your place
in the family of things.

Mary Oliver

ndowsill of Heaven

From an elder and soft-spoken Southern lady who was diminutive in stature and strong in will, and the mother of a childhood friend, came this poem by Thomas Blake. I took comfort in the matter-of-factness of its recommendation –

> *Every morning lean thine arms awhile*
> *Upon the windowsill of Heaven*
> *And gaze upon the Lord.*
> *Then with the vision in thine heart*
> *Turn strong to meet thy day.*

Bird Mindfulness

T his fall morning, after my welcome good night's sleep and first sip of coffee, my kitchen window frames a sight I might have missed on other days. I notice tiny birds perched all over the Japanese lace maple, now an oriental tree of life. The birds are earnest and perky, the tree slender-branched and low over the ground, sheltering, delicate in leaf, resplendent in red and orange.

I wonder what exactly the birds are seeking so determinedly. I wonder what their name is. Grey with crisp white and black markings, they are, little pilgrims just three diminutive inches long from beak to tailfeather.

Maybe one day I will unearth my bird-book again.

Indian Summer

I ndian summer is a dividend of warmth, time, optimism. Fall is indeed here and winter cold is next, but right now both are deliciously forestalled. All around, people notice this reprieve. "History" is being made. Later, we will say *Remember that fall a few years ago? We were in shirtsleeves in November . . . went to the beach for a picnic.*

On our streets the leaves are mostly still up – illumined reds and golds against a sky bluer than you have ever seen it. But neighbors decide to rake the few downed leaves anyway. There is a peacefulness in local hearts, time for a few more outdoor chores, time to go for a walk in the park after all.

From overhead comes that droney distant sound of a small plane, usually a springtime sound, and always comforting. Birds and squirrels are assiduously at work. Their hoppings and foragings seem no less urgent than on other autumn days; *they* are not fooled. Out in the harbor a few boats still sail. How could they be so lucky?

Night Winds

G ale force winds come at our shores tonight, or so it seems. A mere thirty blustery knots is more likely. I think of ships at sea and boats in harbor and Sound. The wind is building up the seas, I know, and – ashore – bending the tree trunks amazingly and whipping the last of the leaves right off.

Hardy sailors – those whose sea trips bridge the seasons - must be having a time of it. And in our own yards there will be trees down and limbs and twigs pruned by God. Squirrels in high-up summer nests may decide that enough is enough, and come down – reluctantly? – to their fall-winter havens in old logs. And what do the birds do? Sit tight and wait for breakfast; there's no fighting this. I do hear some untimely calls whenever the wind lets up.

It is a *grand* sleep tonight for us in houses, waking to age-old wind-sounds every now and then.

Fox

Tonight, after singing in my church, which is old and white-steepled and set beside a quiet pond, I start home but in moments return for a forgotten jacket. A red fox lopes across the churchyard just near me, eyes gleaming in my car lights, startled and stilled. Hadn't we all gone away for the night?

He is beautiful with his low fluffy body and slender fox-face, and his full straight-out tail. His presence seems an exquisite secret, one of nature's treasures in russet and gold. A gift to me in my thirst.

Island Quality

We forget sometimes. But think of all that we are, Long Island, that is of island quality. We are harbors, steep-sided to the north thanks to glaciers, yet sandy-flat with dune inlets to the south, on our Atlantic side. We are inland hills and rivers from all directions, meandering through woods with great old trees and heading shoreward through ferns.

We are peaceful coves behind steep spits of sand-soil land – coves sheltering boats and swimmers and ferryboats to other places. We are miles and miles of undulating surrounding shore with water grasses, oyster shells, gulls, pebbly-sandy beaches, and mud marshlands full of secrets. We are cold north winds and sweet southerlies, tern-cries and drifty clouds, waves and wavelets. We are docks and jetties and ancient glacial boulders, and quiet tidal shallows with stick-legged wading birds, fishing intently.

By season, we are greenings and splashy boat launchings in spring, dawn fishermen and lobstermen and sailboats all around in summer and fall, and giant piled-up ice chunks with snowy drifts in winter.

With all of that, we are particularly a place for gazing. For marveling at miraculous constructions such as horse-shoe crabs and other water treasures, white-sailed vessels in the offing, dawns and sunsets, children building summer sandcastles, and the million things swimming and growing and thriving at harbor's edge. Not to mention that – like any place on earth with its own natural wonders – we are beautiful solitude at dusk or sunrise, for thinking things over.

Ant

I wonder about the ant I admire in my back yard this morning. He (she?) heads determinedly in one direction, zigzagging to be sure but ultimately aiming somewhere specific.

He takes no apparent note of my dog's moving paw six inches away. A double needle fallen from the nearby Mugo pine is twice an obstacle. The cracks between terrace bricks are ravines. The unevennesses in a brick's surface are definitely to be skirted. I watch, unhurriedly.

The ant is an assiduous little entity, I am thinking, no larger than a peppercorn and twice as thin. How ever does he know what he knows? Like his brethren this particular one is ingeniously constructed, section by section. He digs holes beneath bricks and builds hills grain by grain. He lives for very few seasons, plays his key role in nature, works arduously on his multitude of tasks, drags his wounded friend back home to the hill.

How does he do all this? And what does he think of splattering raindrops? Of loud noises? Of boys' sneakers scuffling anthills? The questions are endless.

I am standing on the seashore. A ship at my side spreads her white sails to the morning breeze and departs for the blue ocean. She is an object of beauty, and I watch her until at length she hangs like a speck of white cloud just where the sea and sky meet.

Then someone at my side says "She's gone!"

Gone where? Gone from my sight, that is all.

She is just as large in mast and hull and spar as she was when she left my sight, and just as able to bear her load of living freight to the place of her destination. Her diminished size is in me - not in her.

And just at that moment when someone at my side says "There, she is gone!", there are other eyes watching her coming, and other voices ready to take up the glad shout "Here she comes!"

And that is Living, not Dying.

- Anonymous

From memorial services, St. John's Church

Winter

The Tree of Lights

The Tree of Lights is offered to all present at a Hospice Celebration near Westhampton Beach, Long Island, each December. Tucked all over the tree are little red wooden hearts, each with a beloved name, hung on silky red ribbons. The Tree of Lights gathering is a time for remembering, being grateful, healing after a death. The words spoken at this celebration, drawn from many different faiths, are inexpressibly comforting. This quotation is from the Litany of Remembrance, in the Jewish New Union Prayer Book.

I still remember, I will forever remember, the solace I felt in hearing these encompassing words.

> *In the rising of the sun and in its going down,*
> > *we remember them.*
> *In the blueness of the sky and in the warmth of summer,*
> > *we remember them.*
> *In the rustling of leaves and in the beauty of autumn,*
> > *we remember them.*
> *In the beginning of the year and when it ends,*
> > *we remember them.*

When we are weary and in need of strength,
*   we remember them.*
When we are lost and sick at heart,
*   we remember them.*
When we have joys we yearn to share,
*   we remember them.*
So long as we live, they too shall live, for they are
*   now a part of us, as we remember them.*

Whither From Here

At a sad time that has become a healing time, everywhere I look there are offerings that answer my question: "Whither from here?"

Offerings of hope – yesterday, for instance, I saw a fieldful of ewes and new lambs – a proverbial and renewing sight, before my very eyes.

Of secret, beloved enterprise – today I saw a rock garden of grey-green dusty miller and sunny daffodils tucked down in the very end of an outdoor rapid transit track. I will never learn who created the garden, but its loveliness will stay with me.

Of insight – a reference in David Guterson's book *Snow Falling on Cedars*: a prayer for "deliverance from grief in the course of time."

Of bright flowers – for many months after my sister's death, coming home, I found small bouquets or cheery pots of streptocarpus or cyclamen on my doorstep, each with a note bringing love.

Of connections between ordinary mind today (my own) and brilliant mind a century ago (Tennyson's, in his poem "Ulysses," given to me by a friend) –

> *I am part of all I have met . . .*
> *How dull it is to pause, to make an end*
> *To rust unburnish'd, not to shine in use! . . .*

Death closes all; but something ere the end,

Some work of noble note, may yet be done . . .

The light begins to twinkle from the rocks;

The long day wanes: the slow moon climbs: the deep

Moans round with many voices. Come, my friends,

'Tis not too late to seek a newer world. . . .

Tho' much is taken, much abides. . . .

All Is Well

   This ancient poem came from a friend who found it on a card she mailed to a needful person years ago. She had kept a typewritten copy and now sent it to me. Another friend wished to give it to her father at a time of sadness, so keyboarded my copy and printed it out with a lovely border, and gave a copy back to me.

   One year later – to my happy astonishment – I came upon it again in a sixth-century cathedral in Bangor, Wales, while traveling with my son. It is by Canon Henry Scott-Holland, 1847-1913 –

> *Death is nothing at all.*
> *I have only slipped into the next room.*
> *I am I and you are you.*
> *Whatever we were to each other that we are still.*
>
> *Call me by my old familiar name,*
> *speak to me in the easy way which you always used.*
> *Put no difference into your tone;*
> *wear no forced air of solemnity or sorrow.*

Laugh as we always laughed,
at the little jokes we enjoyed together.

Let my name be ever the household word it always was.
Let it be spoken without effect,
without the ghost of a shadow on it.

Life means all that it ever meant. It is the same as it ever was;
there is absolutely unbroken continuity.

What is this death but a negligible accident;
why should I be out of mind because I am out of sight?
I am but waiting for you, for an interval,
somewhere very near,
just around the corner.
All is well.

Morning

This morning, dawn seems absolutely backwards – with hope coming from an uncustomary quarter. In the east I see only somber greyness and trees tossing in wind so deep that it riffles puddles too.

But to the west, I see clearing and the beginnings of brightness. I have never seen that exchange of compass points before. Perhaps I have never so needed to as now.

Crossing the Street

This morning, soon after learning that someone I love is gravely troubled, I see a beautiful sight downtown in our historic village. There, a man whose disability makes him childlike receives help, crossing the street, from an elderly lady. She takes his hand. He smiles his thanks.

Later with gladdening heart I decide to water my neglected sunroom plants. What do I discover? That in the new light of lengthening January days, my cyclamen has set luscious buds beneath the canopy of its leaves, unobserved until now.

I guess the two sights, the street-crossers and the cyclamen, have been saved for this right moment.

Long Island December

Out for a walk I first see bleak black trees, commiseration for my soul. But then I see swans pure white and perfectly content while wintry winds toss everything around, and fancy overtakes me. Where are they from, these winds? Did they cross the Atlantic? Or swoop down from Boston? Slide over Arctic glaciers?

Inside, later, I see candles, singers, love-smiles. I think of firesides and of people who must travel on cold oceans today. I am in a church at Christmas time, but my mind also visits my Island's marsh, sand dune, and numberless other harbor peripheries. Safe haven, here.

Forsythia Is Fooled

I cy blue sunrise . . . lovely. Peace wished for . . . peace received. I am thinking, before sleep, about gifts. We have had a spate of shirt-sleeve January days in the East this year. We have all savored the ease of no ice and lighter jackets, yet we have also felt not quite right about it.

Now is also a time of earthquake in Japan, flood in California, unethical politics, and trials of all kinds. Things are generally upside down.

In our yards the forsythia is fooled – and snowdrops, rhododendron buds, jonquil shoots are fooled too. The beloved signs of spring are here yet not rightly so. Passersby worry together for these faithful buds and shoots.

Perhaps the message is that nature will yet again get through all this, and human nature too. A reassuring thought!

Sun Up

I am glad for the work I need to do today – writing things, editing things, all in a welcoming local library quiet and well away from telephone and fax. So I will go out for a run, hug the dog, and then go out the door to that peaceful place.

Outside my house I see that it is a Richard Scarry kind of morning: sun well up in the sky, school buses bright yellow, trucks delivering things, neighbors waving hello from the sidewalks, and, jarringly, mysteriously, an "advance life support" ambulance down the street, with all eventually well.

My neighborhood is a microcosm of the world, a reminder that, mostly, we are by kindly instinct each other's keepers. I carry these microcosm reminders into the library with me as if in a book-bag, shoulder slung, comfortable, comforting.

Snow in March

C rocuses – what plucky, cheery things they are. I see a blue-purple one, besieged just like the rest of us with one more persistent snowfall after a legion of them. (This whiteness now is so pristine it would have thrilled us in November, but it is unwelcome now.) The blue-purple crocus is snow-hidden all over again but still aims up toward light. A lesson for us all.

*"What we have once enjoyed and deeply loved we can never lose,
for all that we love deeply becomes part of us."*

– Helen Keller

*"In the depth of winter, I finally learned that within me there lay
an invincible summer."*

– Albert Camus

Spring

Skateboarding

Soon after learning of my sister's illness, and after offering to keep her in prayers, a friend came up to me at choir rehearsal and announced: "I took your sister skateboarding with me today. We had a fine time." What a lovely thought! I told my sister and she thought so too.

Later, not quite two years after her death, I took my sister with me in my mind too. We went shopping for treasures in elegant Neiman Marcus, driving the Pacific coast, gazing up awestruck at the Navy's Blue Angels in their air show over the northern California hills. It was a beautiful trip we once took together and now took together again, the memory clear as a bell, possible only after the passage of time.

Easter Letter

Not too long ago I came upon a copy of this letter to my daughter at Easter time, when she was newly on her own after college and still in the midst of uncertainty. It seems true for us all –

This letter is a "keep-your-faith-it's-a-difficult-time" letter, putting in writing my recent spoken words. It is not bad at all to be in wondering time. It is good. And it is far better now than years later when you are not free to act on your dreams.

It is important – to you and to the world – for you to have dreams and to seek them. And to spend your working hours at something that pleases you. Why? Because truly it is the journey that counts, not the destination. It matters that you find treasures in every day.

The secret is, it is in your hands to find the treasures in your day. So think of Easter each year, starting now, as a time for beginning new things. Perhaps that is the source of Easter's gentle appeal to people: the chance, the encouragement, to begin again. Here is a quote my friend Nancy sent me; I do not know its source: "Whatsoever things are true, honest, just, pure, lovely, of good report, think on these things."

My very dear daughter you are a non-pareil, and that is lovely and difficult. You run deep. You are instinctively of cheery outlook and things not yet clear will become clear in time, and bring you joy. Have faith!

Samuel's Poem

A friend, knowing my affection both for words and for her nine-year-old son Samuel, sent me this poem so that I could share her delight and pride. Samuel gave his mother permission to send the poem to me. I wonder if the Baseball Player is his gentle-mannered grandfather, with whom I sing in the church choir –

The Baseball Player

There once was a man
That had been playing baseball for 70 years!
He is too old now.
He would love to play
But he is just
*   too old.*
He still goes to baseball games
And plays baseball with his grandson
And tells him he might be the best
*   baseball player*
In the world
*   some day. . . .*

Where Is Your Garden, Anyway?

In response to questions of mine, and to my yet-unfulfilled wish to have a garden, came a care package of pleasing quotations with this accompanying note —

I've been thinking about your question: "Where is my sister's spirit?" Some days I think I would say as calmly as possible: gone. But other days I know I would reassure you: not gone at all, just . . . somewhere else.

Because I've been thinking these things, I've assembled a care package for you . . . we will have lots of good stuff to talk about on morning walks or late afternoon cookie-fests or even just staring blankly at the big empty space where your garden, as yet, isn't. Maybe we can wonder: where is your garden anyway? It has existed in my mind ever since you told me about your wish for it, and surely exists in yours, as a dream and a need. And one of these days it will be there.

Meanwhile, your garden has a sort of existence which is invisible but powerful. A little like the question of where your sister is, in reverse, perhaps.

Silken Ties

J ust as spring fulfills its first annual promises, a friend reminds me of a line of a poem, a beautiful line. The words encompass all of us – the ones of us in tiny houses and the ones in those mansions along Long Island's steep shores, today and generations ago, and in other of the world's places and times as well.

The line is by Robert Frost and refers to the interconnections of all things on earth, including two people who love each other, as "countless silken ties of love and thought." Isn't that grand?

April

I can see the saddest thing this morning: rows of daffodils bent over entirely, sturdy green stems looking uncustomarily weary, yellow heads resting on a brick pathway beside them. Sudden cold has knocked the flowers down as if by nature's firing squad. It is a desolate sight on a grey day.

Later, after my day of details and ordinary inconsequential acts, I see the flowers at sundown. They are still bowed down some, but their yellow heads are well away from the bricks by now. Each seems demure rather than ruined, and on the way toward "laughing and dancing in the breeze" – as Wordsworth says is much more fitting for spring.

What an amazing engineering feat *that* has been!

Rushing By

Today, rushing for deadlines threatens to do me in. It is not a collision of cars, this near miss, or anything so dramatic or tangible. It is a collision of two wills within me – one pressing for silly miracles in the workplace, the other urging a more introspective and nourishing time. It is a classic sort of standoff. The day's ordinary errands save me.

To begin, my village welcomes me with its shops, rewarding my instinct for procrastination, my yearning for calm.

The line at the local drugstore is short but snail slow. The cheery lady at the cash register trails off to weigh some Easter chocolates for my predecessor in line, then at my turn smiles and wishes me a lovely day – and means it. Her way is contagious. My way softens into hers.

Next, a printer down the block commiserates about my deadlines. He mentions his wish to see his children's soccer games, so not opening his shop on Saturdays despite the urgings of time and economics. It is a dear moment between vendor and client.

Not too much later a friend finds Main Street's trees wonderful to look upon and tells me so – flowering pears with their earliest April shoots and snowy blossoms. And nearby against the sky, traceries of the branches of bigger trees show promise too. My steps slow into strolling. I notice the fine-mortared old brick facades above the shopfronts.

On the way home I pass greening lawns, teenage boys riding bikes up steep hills effortlessly, with their baseball caps on backward. Sunlight lazily slants its tree-shadows across the road. And I see schoolboys standing together casually with lacrosse sticks and backpacks, looking down at the stones they are kicking back and forth, and, surely, speaking of girls.

Blessings

S ome weeks ago I was felled by a flu, or something. All night long I felt and was ill, and at one point it was supremely blissful to lie down on the floor rather than try anything more.

For days after, I was capable of just about nothing: I, customarily a joyous, energized soul. No joy, no optimism or kind acts, no achievements of any sort were possible.

But today, little by little my ordinary treasures – as I now perceive them to be – are returning. Chicken soup is manna. Mystery stories hold peace and solace again, crossword puzzles too. Watering my plants, fixing supper, doing laundry, walking (albeit s l o w l y !) around the block – all are becoming possible again. My Work Projects – hitherto sacred priorities – present themselves as afterthoughts, mere pleasing possibilities.

The kaleidoscope of my outlook seems changed now. I think of people who are ill perpetually as I had briefly been, or troubled in other ways. Watering plants or feeding a child or reading a mystery are never even possible for some. Or weeding gardens, or noticing dogwoods with morning light behind their blossoms.

And so, I count my blessings today.

Summer

God Keep You, Dearest

This anonymous quotation was sent by Sybil Stockdale in a letter to her husband Vice Admiral James B. Stockdale, a prisoner of war in Hanoi for more than seven years. I read his extraordinarily beautiful book, *In Love and War,* and wrote to him to tell him of my regard. How sustaining his wife's words must have been for this brave imprisoned man –

> *God keep you, dearest, all this lonely night;*
> *The winds are still,*
> *The moon drops down behind the western hill,*
> *God keep you, dearest, 'til the light.*

Give Me Understanding

These words are from a gentle and sacred song long known to our church choir. They were written by our former choirmaster, himself as gentle as his song. Its harmonies are simple and sweet. For me, after my sister's illness and death, its final lines seemed the perfect sequence for this request –

Father, give me peace.
And, if it be thy will
Give me understanding.

Lord, Slow Me Down

This gift of words came from a friend, older than I by three decades or so, who has the wisest and most generous and optimistic of spirits –

Slow me down, Lord.

Ease the pounding of my heart by the quieting of my mind.

Steady my hurried pace with a vision of the eternal reach of time.

Give me, amid the confusion of the day, the calmness of the everlasting hills.

Break the tensions of my nerves and muscles with the soothing music of the singing streams that live in my memory. Help me to know the magical, restoring power of sleep.

Teach me the art of taking minute vacations – of slowing down to look at a flower, to chat with a friend, to pat a dog, to read a few lines from a good book.

Slow me down, Lord, and inspire me to send my roots deep into the soil of life's enduring values that I may grow toward the stars of my greater destiny.

The Pictures Within You

These words of counsel came from a book called *Guests in My Life* by Elizabeth Watson, who gathered them at a time of terrible loss and offered them to others in her book. The book was lent to me by a loving friend who waited until I was ready to receive it, and the quotation is by the author Ranier Marie Rilke, who, also, was moving through a time of grief.

> *Work of sight is done.*
> *Now do heart work on the pictures within you.*

The Rock Club

T oday is trying to be full of rushes, so as an antidote I will think about a small event that happened the other day at the beach. Early morning light shimmerings through the summer-green pin oak tree in my yard, and mellifluous birdsong, are my surroundings as I think back –

At the beach that other day, at the end of the afternoon, I am caught without book or crossword puzzle while waiting for a friend. So I settle back in my chair for an introspective thought or two. Toes in the sand. A gift of time.

But nearby, two very young boys sit cross-legged, slender-bodied, earnest, pounding rocks upon rocks and making a racket that damages my introspection, or so I believe.

Actually, as I listen, they agree to form a rock club. They sanctify their membership with "Indian rock" paint – a russet stripe to each small palm, from water mixed with the reddish insides of rocks they had split.

Their delight, and their solemnity and innocence at age seven or so, are my memory of this luminescent time.

Good Night's Sleep

Usually, after a good night's sleep, everything is somehow possible again. Yesterday's megrims are dimmed or gone. Optimism has returned. Morning is my time to think of shedding burdens, of changing ways, of daring to do some undone things at last.

Accordingly, this morning, I sit in my chair with flowered cushions, surrounded by windows of early light. I write a long-meant-to love letter to a friend. I water my plants, poor thirsty souls. I sit out in the yard while our cavorting black Labrador Jake shows me his racing and squirrel-finding skills. I wonder what the chittering birds are saying to each other.

I plan my day, mindful that doing fewer things a bit more slowly fills the day wonderfully – in the true sense of that word – instead of frenetically.

Mornings like this make me take a deep breath, and recognize the prayers and songs of the day.

"I will hold you in my thoughts"

J ust a few months after the death of my sister, a "secret" came to me: a friend was newly and seriously ill. Our children had traveled paths that paralleled and parted and now converged, to our shared delight. Our oldests were not much beyond college and starting their independent, hope-laden lives – sent off with celebration.

Within days, the secret about my friend was shared by one caring person with the next, and the next. A wildfire secret, its promise violated thanks to love. So very soon I told it to my children. "Tuck this away," I said. "You may be called upon."

Their young hearts were old enough for sadness, and their wish to give comfort made me weep with gratefulness and mourning. For my sister, for my friend, for us all.

We need each other at moments like this. And isn't it the very dearest thing, therefore, to say to a friend, as another once said to me, "I will hold you in my thoughts."

Fall, & Full Circle

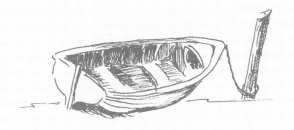

Two Journeys

From a letter to a faraway friend, in thanks for listening when I needed to talk –

It is early in the morning, and I write to tell you of my thankfulness for your cards and calls. It seems as though there are two journeys here – my sister's, and the journey of those left behind. I'll try and send you some of the sweet poems and quotes I have received – your kindly spirit will I believe drink them in. I guess this is "mourning," when you are wisest to talk and cry and putter as seems dearest, and most respectful and comforting.

Brother and Sister

Writing this letter to my two children, who are not children any more, seemed essential after my sister's death. It was soothing advice to offer, as if I were bequeathing a message made of gold.

Care for each other! Make the call . . . write the letter. We are each other's keepers, and between brother and sister like you there is possible a thread of caring finer than all other interconnections you will have. In its length – a lifetime. In its depth – an infinity of shared moments, funny or dear, ordinary, unplanned, uncounted, sustaining.

I write now after the loss of my own sister, grateful for trust and laughter special among all friendships and loves in my life. As one of your parents, and thus one of your teachers, I want to shake your shoulders a little here. Open your eyes today!

You see, there are people in the world who will hurt you on purpose – the Golden Rule neither guides nor touches their lives. And there are people who will hurt you by chance, whether from inadvertence or lack of confidence or care, or simply without endowment to do otherwise. But not your brother, not your sister!

You see, it is honestly the small acts – between brother and sister, between caring friends – that light things up. It is the letter that comes on a low day, the call that somehow comes plumb in the middle of a dark time, that matters most. And small miracles such as these, taken together, will light up your world.

The Time to Say Love

I wrote this letter to a schoolmate – a kitchen-table neighbor in the early grades and a laughing, philosophizing, challenge-meeting friend in our later lives – in thanks for a book and a quote –

You are the dearest person. I feel as though I am beginning an ancient ritual of grieving: "Thank you for giving me love when I most need it" is the message that is so comforting to send back to you.

Your book is a delight and is as welcome as morning sun. Your words and lovely letter yesterday made me cry at the end of a long day, itself a mixture of true "business" work and "friend" work – talking and remembering at a time when that is needed and welcome.

And your specific wish – "I pray that God will soften the hard edges of this for you – with friends who love you and gentle things happening."

What a fine wish . . .

People are being so wonderful to me – not because they knew my sister because most did not. But because they are of good will, and they care for me as I do for them, and they seem to know that now is the time to say love.

Those Who Have Finished Their Work in This Life

After reading my Kindnesses journal, a friend likened it to the prayer below, of which he says: "It is a favorite of mine, and your journal evokes the same wonderful feeling of peace as I apply it to those loved ones of ours who have finished their work in this life." The prayer is a familiar one –

O Lord support us all the day long,
until the shadows lengthen and the evening
comes and the busy world is hushed and the
fever of life is over and our work is done.
Then in thy mercy grant us a safe lodging
and a holy rest and peace at the last.

A Birthday

Today is my birthday. It has been a blessed day, filled with dear acts by dear friends. It has been more full of love than any birthday before, for me.

First a cheery greeting from my husband. Then telephoned wishes from three friends, then a day of work among people of good will.

Amidst the day come calls from my far-away children . . . yellow chrysanthemums on my doorstep from a neighbor . . . fragrant flowers from a beloved shopkeeper and staff . . . my day's song crazily sung by someone on the telephone! . . . and a tiny sparkly present, homemade and wrapped in bright redpink ribbons, from a friend.

Now I have always loved birthdays, mine and everyone else's. But something is different this year. My seasons of sadness bring yearnings for comfort and love. Which seem, lately, to emerge for the silent asking.

October Sunday

On an October Sunday this year, I drift home peacefully after church. Church itself – with singing and a coffee hour afterwards and conversations in sunshine in the parking lot – has been good for the soul. At home, however, afternoon guests are soon to come. Old friends from out of town, the guests are, who have never been to our house, or met our dog, or seen our treasures of family photographs and sentimental objects assembled over time.

Amidst the hurried necessary straightenings there comes a delicious interlude: spruce up the outdoor geraniums in their terra cotta pots. These still blossom in innocent pinks and corals in Indian summer, yet have been neglected amidst the season's rash professional promises.

My discovery? Taking away spent leaves and blooms, slow and steady in friendly Sunday sun and with a blissful disregard for time, I find the yield of an earlier cutting-back of untended plants. I find tiny new geranium leaves sprouted in near-mathematical profusion, along each shortened stem. Kind of like springtime in autumn.

I could so easily have missed it.

Puppies

O h I think it's time!" . . . Hushed observations.

"Yes, I just saw a contraction! Oh, good heavens, here's another one!"

We are watching puppies being born. It is a miracle right there in front of us. My friend's chocolate lab Hazel is having her first litter and the father is our black lab Jake. It is Hazel's own birthday and it is two days before Christmas, after my year filled with sadness and returning joy.

Sure enough, out comes another tiny creature in slick membranous enclosure. Hazel knows precisely what to do. She licks away her puppy's birth surroundings, nibbles to sever the cord, and rolls him back and forth with her cleansing tongue until he glistens and squeaks satisfactorily, ready to join his little siblings to snuggle in, eyes closed, to nurse.

It is all so beautiful. The eve before Christmas Eve.

The Linen Closet

Today I am straightening out the linen closet. It has been forever since I've done this, and the towels are every which way and the sheets piled at odd angles and the wash cloths toppling over. Not to mention the medicines and cold remedies sitting on the little shelves inside the closet, all jumbled together and years and years out of date.

For weeks and months and perhaps even longer I have noticed the jumble of towels and meant to refold them, but their chaos seemed to reflect my own. The moment – the inspired moment when cheeriness and energy conspire – has not come until now.

I find treasures in that closet. Oh, my! Old treasures – baby aspirin, syrupy cough medicines, a receiving blanket, a wash rag in the shape of a bear. My earlier imperfect straightenings have missed these hidden things. My children are taller than I am now; my memories classic. The baby blanket is the palest blue with white stripes, soft flannel. Achingly, gratefully, I remember its many washings and foldings twenty-five years ago. After nursing and changing and playing I would wearily tuck our tiny daughter away under this very blanket, all snug around the edges of her cradle. It stood for sweet sleep and orderliness, the blanket did, as I learned my way in mothering.

Summer Church

Darkness to dawn . . . It is an age-old journey, and now I am a traveler. Whole years of seasons have come and gone, since a death that still astounds me. It is summer again. Life has gone right on – laughter and tears, hope and despair, spring blossoms and winter ice and round again, everything the same as always.

But of course it is not the same at all. Sad moments still come sometimes, surprising and intense like summer storms. Why today, now? Perhaps it is the news-hawker's headlines – dispiriting, dwelling terrier-like on mistakes and frailties, so often boding ill. Or perhaps it is just ordinary weariness after an impassioned week of work. Does it matter why?

What matters for me, actually, is a glimmer within this particular Sunday morning. There does always seem to be a glimmer now. It is a radiance that I surely never doubt – I just forget it, or cannot see it, at low times.

It is the radiance of possibility, joy, the kindnesses of friends. It is the life-gratefulness of which Alan Paton wrote: "Something within me is waking from long sleep, and I want to live and move again. . . . I have not told myself to be thankful, I just am so." And it is a radiance that always seems to find me. I must teach myself to count on it.

For this morning, seeking a lightening of spirit, I write down a list of losses and then across the page a list of kindred souls and ordinary miracles that have not left my life. The list of losses is short yet nearly overwhelming. But the list of kindred souls and happenstance is long, so long that it brims with reassurance.

Minutes later, outdoors with Sunday morning's second cup of coffee, I notice young petunias in bold pinks and purples, soft-petaled and lush in the huge old grey stone pot beside my chair. Across the yard, early sun just touching its tallest branches, I see that our young plum tree has quietly produced tiny plump fruits – its first ever.

Journey Through
The Seasons of Grief

After my sister's death I sought a way out of sadness but did not find it for the longest while. My journal of rage and gratefulness, my sustaining talks with friends, my heightened delight in the ordinary details of my surroundings – of the churchyard fox, the rock club, my imaginary garden – helped for the moment. But sadness always settled in again like mist.

Then one plain day, perhaps in response to my wishings for "the peace of God that passeth all understanding," two recent chance remarks came into my mind for mulling over, and sadness simply lifted and was gone.

One remark was from a counselor, who said, "I hope that one day you will be able to say: I had a sister, and I lost her, and from her I learned how to have beloved friends."

The other was from a friend whose daughter and mine have been friends since childhood, and with whom I have long felt a quiet connection. At dinner one night she said to me, offhandedly, "I am truly sorry at your sadness. I can't even imagine it. You see, I never had a sister to lose."

And so in my journey through the seasons of grief, at long last, sadness has given way to gratefulness and understanding. Tears still come sometimes, surprising me at being so deep and unforeseen. But I am different now, richer of mind and spirit in this my sixtieth year, wiser sometimes, more patient, more grateful. And when I slow down or take a mindful glance I am, endlessly, nourished by the small wonders of the day. Truly, all is well. I wish the same for all of us – in mountain or plain, desert or forest, inland or coast, in all our seasons.

- Terry Walton
October 2001

Journal of Kindnesses

_____

_____

_____

_____

_____

_____

_____

_____

_____

_____

_____

Also by Terry Walton –

Cold Spring Harbor Daybook

Cold Spring Harbor . . .
Rediscovering History in Streets and Shores
(for Cold Spring Harbor Whaling Museum)

kindnesses